Lexington, Kentucky
Past & Present

Alma Wynelle Deese
Photography by John Malick

Schiffer Publishing Ltd®
4880 Lower Valley Road Atglen, Pennsylvania 19310

Dedication

To Judge J.W. Deese, who encouraged the beginning of this book but did not live to see it completed. He died March 3, 2008, after 42 years of marriage to the author.

Disclaimer

The prices listed in this book were the prices paid for the postcards over a long period of collecting Lexington, Kentucky view cards in an ever changing world. The prices listed in this book range from the earliest to the more current price according to the author's observation. These prices were given only to help the beginning collectors rather than for any steadfast rule.

Price Guide

There are many excellent books on pricing old postcards, including some by Allman, Miller, Woods, and Others, as listed in the bibliography. These books identify different categories of old postcards and show how each category shares a range of prices.

The Lexington postcards fit a general category of views and have been referred to as the core of the hobby. That general category shares a price range that varies according to several of the following factors: age and location. The older a postcard is, usually it is less available and more expensive to obtain. A local collector will generally want anything connected with their favorite town and purchasing a view in that town can result in local competition and higher prices.

Another factor in postcard pricing is the desirability of the subject matter. Views that are static or buildings that never change are less desirable than ones that occur only once. A fourth factor is related to the quality of the picture and/or focus. A fuzzy picture has less value than one in clear color. Yet, there are always exceptions especially when the subject matter of a postcard has personal meaning to the purchaser.

Supply and demand is another factor in pricing postcards. Early Lexington, Kentucky view cards are not as plentiful as those in St. Petersburg, Florida because tourism came early to Florida. Yet, Lexington cards are more plentiful than Mississippi ones because there were more early ones produced of Kentucky. Early postcards of Mississippi are still very scarce while they have a limited demand. There have been no recent postcard shows in Mississippi while Florida frequently has postcard shows, especially in the winter.

A final factor in the pricing of old postcards is the recognition that inflation and time will influence the prices. Generally, early view cards have increased in price as the demand have increased and the supply is limited due to their age. While postcards purchased years ago have mostly increased in price, the degree of increase is dependent upon the previously mentioned factors. Many early collectors have become dealers today while their old inventories can be priced as they wish. Then, there are the collectors who purchased old postcards like art, expecting them to appreciate in value with time. Like any investor, the more knowledge one gains, the better the investment.

Library of Congress Control Number: 2009928943

Covers and book designed by: Bruce Waters
Type set in Zurich Bt

ISBN: 978-0-7643-3290-6
Printed in China

Schiffer Books are available at special discounts for bulk purchases for sales promotions or premiums. Special editions, including personalized covers, corporate imprints, and excerpts can be created in large quantities for special needs. For more information contact the publisher:

Published by Schiffer Publishing Ltd.
4880 Lower Valley Road
Atglen, PA 19310
Phone: (610) 593-1777; Fax: (610) 593-2002
E-mail: Info@schifferbooks.com

For the largest selection of fine reference books on this and related subjects, please visit our web site at **www.schifferbooks.com**
We are always looking for people to write books on new and related subjects. If you have an idea for a book please contact us at the above address.

This book may be purchased from the publisher.
Include $5.00 for shipping.
Please try your bookstore first.
You may write for a free catalog.

In Europe, Schiffer books are distributed by
Bushwood Books
6 Marksbury Ave.
Kew Gardens
Surrey TW9 4JF England
Phone: 44 (0) 20 8392 8585; Fax: 44 (0) 20 8392 9876
E-mail: info@bushwoodbooks.co.uk
Website: www.bushwoodbooks.co.uk

Contents

Acknowledgements

Harold Barker has provided historical research and consultation for this book. He worked with the Lexington-Fayette Urban County Government for 33 years. He managed, preserved and made available Archives or records of Lexington and Fayette County Government. He is now part time with the Lexington History Museum. His knowledge and resources were invaluable to finishing this book. Two other people deserve special thanks for providing access to their Lexington post card collections: Peggy Brown and Bill Arvin both have lived in Lexington for many years and have collected postcards of the area. They have been valuable resources through their knowledge and helpfulness to the authors, typical of how postcard collectors help each other.

Introduction

A map of the city of Lexington has been divided into eight sections to delineate the eight chapters in this book. Four Chapters focus on the major streets: Broadway North, Broadway South, East Main and West Main. The other four chapters cover the respective east and west sides of North and South Broadway. This dissection of the city helps the author to focus on the past and present views of the structures, while identifying their locations within the city.

This Introduction includes a mixture of postcards that are important to understanding Lexington's history. A postcard with the poem "In Kentucky" has a unique history starting in Lexington, when the author, Judge James H. Mulligan, introduced it in February of 1902, as part of a banquet for members of the Kentucky legislature at the Phoenix Hotel. That event is described in Chapter 8, with postcards of the Phoenix Hotel.

The poem was first seen on a postcard published by Wrenn and King and reported by the local newspaper in August 3, 1907, as "the poem beautifully printed in post card form which is having a ready sale by Wrenn and King, the enterprising stationers of this city."

Wrenn and King were located at 278 W. Main Street in Lexington, and a postcard of W. Main Street show in Chapter 7 shows their advertising on a building at their location. This publisher produced many early postcards of Lexington, many of which are shown in this book.

The following postcard published by Wrenn and King with the poem "In Kentucky" was mailed on June 12, 1912.

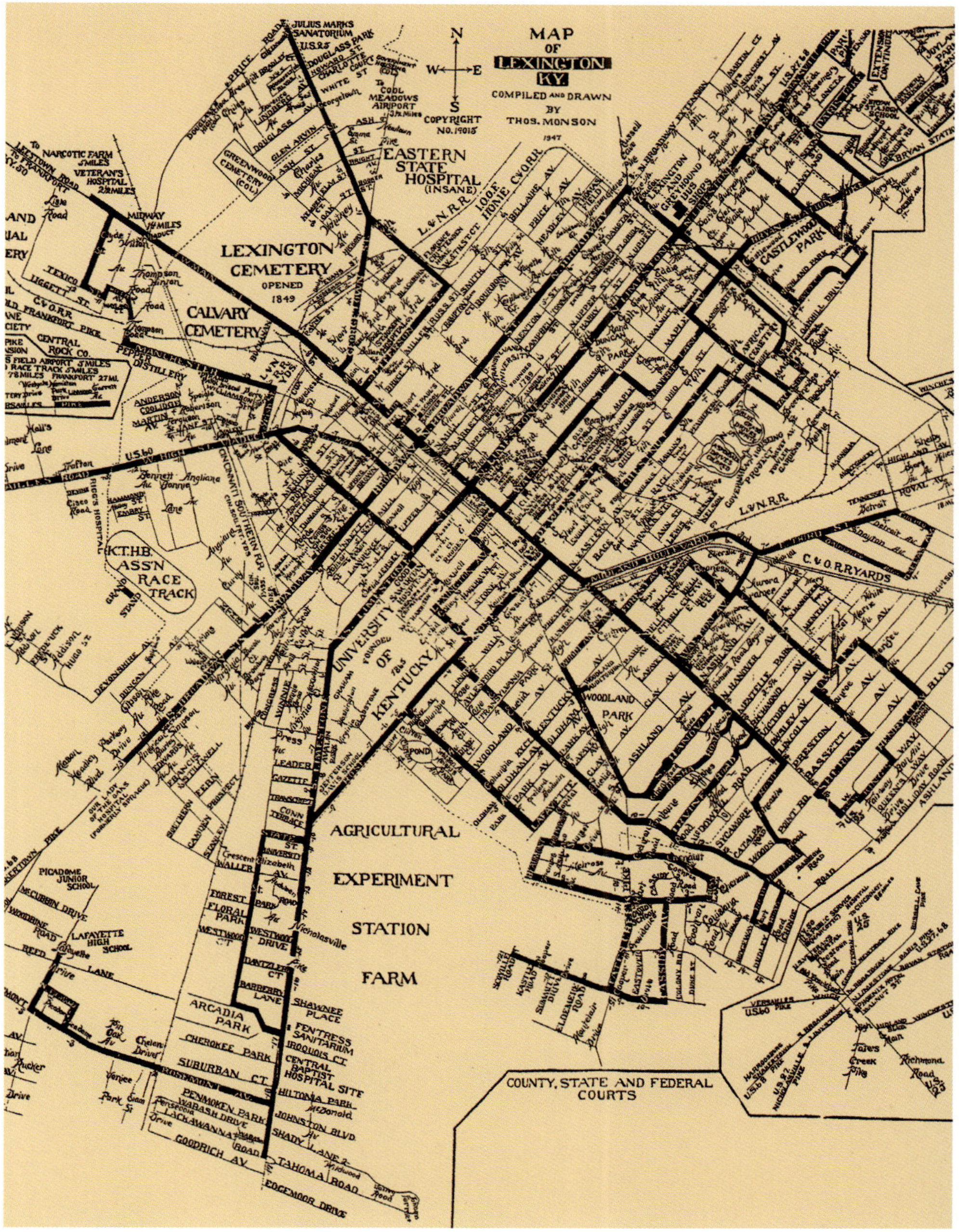

The next three postcards show how that poem was printed by three publishers on postcards. The publisher Curteich added pictures of a Kentucky Colonel and horses in their Kentucky series included with the "In Kentucky" poem.

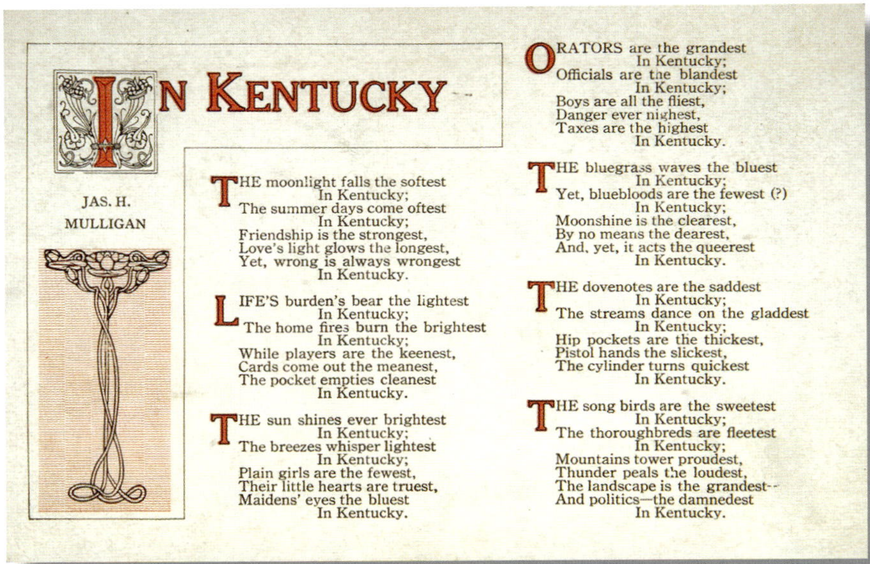

"IN KENTUCKY" postcard published by Wrenn and King, Lexington, Ky. $3-4

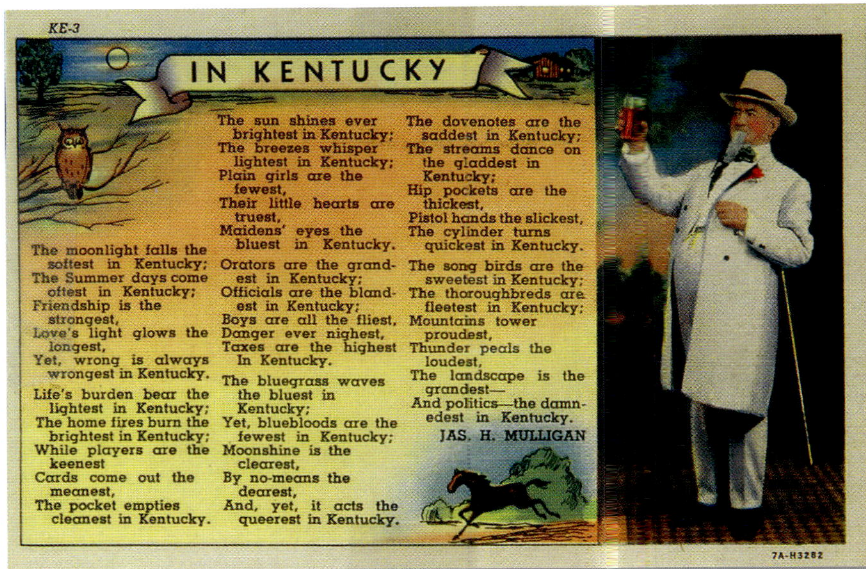

"IN KENTUCKY" postcard published by Curtech, Chicago, Il. *On loan*

E. C. Kropp Co. publishers of Milwaukee, Wisconsin, included views of High Bridge, Kentucky, and the State Capitol along with the poem "In Kentucky."

"IN KENTUCKY" postcard published by E.C. Kropp Co. Milwaukee, Wis. $1-2

Another publisher used other scenes unique to Kentucky on their "In Kentucky" poem postcard. It was mailed December 19, 1944.

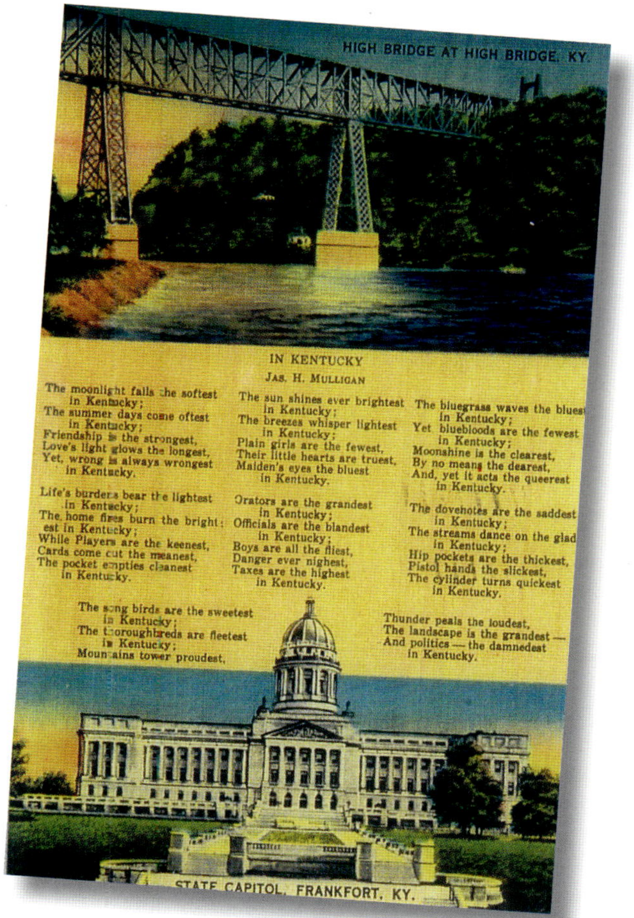

"IN KENTUCKY" postcard published in USA. *On loan*

One Lexington postcard location was difficult to confirm; it is believed to be the Kentucky Central Railroad Depot at Short and Georgetown Street. One Depot was built in 1871 and ownership changed in 1891 to the Louisville & Nashville Railroad. By 1882, the earlier depots were abandoned. This postcard was made around 1900, and often older pictures were added to postcards. This depot may have been important to the early city, but it is not mentioned in early histories.

The first Kentucky Central Railroad Depot at Short and Georgetown Streets. *On loan*

CHAPTER ONE
NORTH LEXINGTON

On North Broadway toward U.S. 68 north and 27

North Broadway was first laid out in 1780 as Main Cross Street. It was the main north-south axis bisecting the original eighteen block of lots composing Lexington. The Street was intended to grow in either direction. The name was changed to Broadway Street in the middle nineteenth century. The current church located on the southwest corner of Broadway and Second Street is the Broadway Christian Church. In January, 1970, the church celebrated 100 years at that location. This Church is where John Malick, the photographer for this book, photographed his first wedding at the age of 15. He was too young to drive, so the groom picked him up and both the groom and bride took him home after the wedding. John did obtain a driver's license at age 16 and continued to photograph weddings in Lexington for forty-five years.

The current church on the southwest corner of Broadway and Second Street. The Broadway Christian Church.

A postcard of the Broadway Christian Church before it burned in 1916. $3-4

A postcard of the Broadway Christian Church shows round arches, entrances in the front corners, and stonework detailed by a color contrast. It has a round tower over the square entrance vestibule with a large wheel window in the steeped pitched front gable. The building burned in 1916 and another was built. Earlier, on this southwest corner of Second Street, stood the First Presbyterian Church of 1808; the Broadway Christian Church was built in 1891.

The grounds where The College of the Bible once stood between 3rd and 4th streets on North Broadway. The College of the Bible was part of the Kentucky University. Transylvania Universitynow occupies the area; the College of the Bible building is gone.

The current location where the College of the Bible stood on North Broadway.

A wider view on north Broadway, this photo shows what is now Transylvania University and several buildings. After the Civil War, Morrison Hall and the College of the Bible buildings became part of the Kentucky University, and which became in 1908 Transylvania University.

A wider view on the corner of North Broadway and 3rd Street, showing Transylvania University and Morrison Hall.

This postcard shows the College of the Bible that was built in 1895, as a large, three-story brick building with a tower facing Broadway Street.

A postcard of the College of the Bible. $3-4

This 1910 postcard shows a wider view of The College of the Bible, Morrison Hall, and the Carnegie Science Hall on the right. The Science Hall was completed in the fall of 1908 when Andrew Carnegie started a matching sum to construct the facility. It had well-equipped chemical-physical and biological laboratories with a museum for the display of geological and zoological specimens. Morrison Hall in the middle, was completed in 1833, while the building on the left has been identified as the Alumni Gymnasium, completed in 1894.

This postcard shows a wider view of the College of the Bible, Morrison Hall and the Carnegie Science Hall. $3-4

In 1950, the College of the Bible moved to a new campus across town on South Limestone Street, opposite the University of Kentucky. At the school's 100th anniversary in 1965, its name was changed to the Lexington Theological Seminary and it continues at that location. A picture and postcard of the newer facility is in Chapter 5.

A 1960s postcard of the Mitchell Fine Arts Center at Transylvania College when it was reported to have a large Auditorium, a 250 seat Theater, a gallery, a student center and bookstore. It was opened in 1966 as one of the newer buildings at Transylvania University.

A postcard of the Mitchell Fine Arts Center at Transylvania College. $1-3

A current picture of the Mitchell Fine Arts Center at Transylvania University.

Hamilton Female College was opened in 1869 by James M. Hocker, following an ample gift to the school by William Hamilton. A three-story building had a basement, gabled pavilions, a verandah at the center, and wings on both sides. An octagonal cupola occupied the center of the roof. This postcard, dated April 13, 1905, shows the view from North Broadway near Fifth Street. On May 5th, 1910, the College had the 41st annual Commencement exercises held at the Opera House, as it had done the previous years.

A current picture at the location of the Hamilton Female College.

A postcard of Hamilton Female College, from North Broadway near Fifth Street. $3-5

This postcard shows a side view of the Hamilton College. It started as Hocker College and the name was changed in 1877 to Hamilton College. In 1914, Hamilton College Was consolidated with Bourbon College in Paris, Kentucky. By 1962, the building had been razed and the grounds were to be converted into an athletic field.

A side view of the Hamilton College location.

This postcard shows a colored view of the Hamilton College. From 1920 to 1962, this college served as a junior college operated by Transylvania University and a girls' dormitory. It was leveled in 1962.

A postcard showing a colored view of Hamilton College. $3-4

Another view of the Hamilton College location on North Broadway Street.

A colored view of Hamilton College. *On loan*.

Current homes on North Broadway.

An article in the local newspaper on July 15, 1906, stated that a petition of prominent men living on Broadway had plans for the street to be converted into "one of the finest of driveways." A petition was made to Mayor Combs asking him to pave Broadway, both north and south, with an asphalt pavement.

A postcard view of homes on North Broadway. *On loan*.

Homes that appear on North Broadway are shown. The next postcard appears to be similar, however there are many old beautiful homes on North Broadway and grown trees make it difficult to identify each home.

Chapter Two

NORTH-EAST LEXINGTON

East of North Broadway and North of East Main Street

At the northwest corner of Church and Mill Streets, this original building is being used by the Lexington Arts and Cultural Council, The Lexington Ballet and Philharmonic Companies.

Another current picture of the northwest corner of Church and Mill Streets shows the location of the Lexington Arts and Cultural Council, including the Ballet and Philharmonic Companies.

The following postcard shows the Y.M.C.A. building at the northwest corner of Church and Mill Streets. A newspaper article on Nov. 7, 1883 stated that a gymnasium was opened at Mill and Church Streets. Another article on February 1904 reported that a new Y.M.C.A. building as erected on the NW corner of Church and Mill. The men's organization vacated the building in August, 1932, and sold it six years later to the Y.W.C.A.

The current northwest corner at Church and Mill Streets.

A postcard of the Y.M.C.A. building at the northwest corner of Church and Mill Streets. $2-4

A current picture features Broadway and Mill on the north side of Short Street. Notice the old building to the right, which may not have been part of the old Hotel Reed and is now used for offices.

The current northwest corner of Church and Mill Streets.

An inside view shows the reading room at the Y.M.C.A. building at the northwest corner of Church and Mill Streets.

The reading room at the Y.M.C.A. building at the northwest corner of Church and Mill Streets. *On loan*.

Broadway and Mill on the north side of Short Street.

A postcard of the Hotel Reed identifyies the proprietors as being the Hart Brothers. Earlier it was known as the Ashland House and the original building was erected in 1873. It was located at 315-317 W. Short Street. This 1908 Hotel Reed claimed to be on the "American Plan of $2.00 and $2.50. It later became The Hotel Drake. Notice a building to the right that did not appear to be part of the old hotel.

A postcard of the Hotel Reed located at 315-317 W. Short Street. $2-4

A current picture taken between Broadway and Mill on the north side of Short Street shows the place as a parking lot.

Another picture between Broadway and Mill on the north side of Short Street .

A current picture shows the north side of Short Street, at #315-317 West Short Street. Notice the old building on the right.

The north side of Short Street, at #315-317 W. Short Street.

A pretty postcard of the Hotel Drake advertising moderate prices.

A postcard of the Hotel Drake. *On loan*.

A postcard showing the Drake Hotel at 315-317 W. Short Street. The postcard was sent in 1930; the Drake Hotel was demolished in 1961 for a parking lot.

A current picture shows Short Street between Mill and Broadway, the old location of the Drake Hotel.

A postcard showing the Drake Hotel at 315-317 W. Short Street. $4-6

Short Street between Mill and Broadway, the location of the Drake Hotel.

A postcard showing the dining room at the Hotel Drake. *On loan.*

A local newspaper article on October 11, 1930 stated that the Drake Cafeteria was opened this day featuring both cafeteria and table service at popular prices. The new cafeteria occupies the quarters where the Tip Toe Inn was formerly located, but that section of the building was remodeled and refinished for this dining room's opening.

This northeast corner of Mill and Short Streets has a long history of various commercial businesses, including Charles Wickliffe's tavern at Mill and Short in 1816. J.B. Simrall, the Mayor of Lexington had a drugstore at this location in 1896.

This early postcard shows an east view of the second tallest building in Lexington completed in 1905. It was located on the site of David Sayre's Bank, the northeast corner of Mill and Short Streets. It was called The Security Trust and Safety Vault Company. Notice the horses and carriages on the north side.

A current picture of the northeast corner of Mill and Short Streets.

The Security Trust and Safety Vault Company Building at the northeast corner of Mill and Short Streets. $4-6

The current northeast corner of Mill and Short Streets.

A postcard sent in 1918 shows Short Street with the Security Trust Company building in the far distance, while the McClelland Building is closer. A Smith-Watkins Hardware building was identified on the far right side, while the firehouse was located on the far left side. The upside-down flag is hard to explain.

A current picture of the north side of Short and Mill Streets shows the same building that was called The Security Trust Co.

A postcard shows the north-east corner of Mill and Short Streets, with the Security Trust Company building. $4-6

A current picture of the north side of Short Street from Mill to Limestone.

This 1908 view on Short Street shows the Security and Trust Co. at Mill Street. Notice the carriages and people.

A postcard view of the Security and Trust Company on Short Street. $3-6

A current view looking east on Short Street towards Limestone. The building at Upper and Short Streets is the McClelland Building, originally with 5 stories, in 1905. It became a seven-story building, as seen in this view.

A current east view on Short Street.

The east view of Short Street can be seen in this postcard while the direction, west, was incorrectly labeled by the postcard publishers. The McClelland Building and others are on the southeast side of Upper and Short Streets, with the back part of the Court house on the southwest corner.

An east view of Short Street. *On loan*.

A current picture of the corner of Limestone and Short Streets shows two newer Court Buildings. These provide facilities for the Criminal and Civil Courts.

The current view of the southeast corner of Limestone and Short Streets.

An inside view of the Kaufman Clothing Company is seen around the 1930s on the corner of Limestone and Short Streets. Earlier, that corner was occupied by Wheelers Furniture Store. Articles in the local newspaper as early as 1896 reported about the Kaufman Clothing Company. In April 1907, the Kaufman Clothing Company was reported to be the annual spring opening of Lexington's biggest store. By 1911, Kaufmans Clothing Co. had made improvements on West Main Street making it not only the largest but one of the handsomest stores in Kentucky. By 1950, the original owner had sold out to James Strauss and preparations for remodeling were announced.

An inside postcard view of the Kaufman Clothing Company. *On loan*.

A current picture of what is now 237 N Limestone.

An earlier view of the Baugh & Garner Furniture Company at 237 North Limestone Street that had trucks to make deliveries. A local newspaper article, dated July 20, 1940, stated that the firm of Baugh and Garner completed 18 years of successful merchandising at the North Limestone building. They considered themselves the leading Central Kentucky furniture merchants.

A postcard view of the Baugh & Garner, Inc. at 237 North Limestone Street. *On loan*.

Currently the U.S. District Court's Federal Building is located on the northeast corner of Barr and Limestone Streets.

The U.S. Post Office opened on the Barr and Limestone Streets corner on December 9, 1934. The U.S. District Courts occupied the 2nd and 3rd floors.

The Federal Building on Barr and Limestone Streets.

An early postcard view of the Federal Building.

The Greyhound Bus Terminal was located at 219 East Short Street from 1948 to 1970. It is currently used by the Central Christian Church.

A current view of 219 East Short Street.

A postcard view of the Greyhound Bus Terminal at 219 East Short Street. $1-3

A postcard view of the Greyhound Bus Terminal at 219 East Short Street. Previously, the Greyhound Bus Station was located at 244 East Main and it moved to 240 North Limestone from 1971 to 1986. It has recently moved to 477 New Circle Road, N W.

The Sayre School is still present on North Limestone Street opposite Second Street, and it provides coeducational classes from first through twelfth grades.

The Sayre School on North Limestone Street.

A postcard showing Sayre College on North Limestone opposite Second Street. $1-3

This postcard shows Sayre College on North Limestone opposite Second Street. It was opened in 1854 as the Transylvania Female Seminary and moved to its present location in 1855.

Another current picture of Sayre School located on North Limestone opposite Second Street.

The current view of a building at Sayre School.

An earlier postcard view depicts Sayre Institute on North Limestone before the driveways were paved.

An early postcard view of Sayre Institute on North Limestone. *On loan*.

The building at 601 North Limestone is believed to be the location of Walker's Ice Cream. It is now a bar. The Lexington City Directory identified the Walker's Ice Cream and Confectionary building at this location from 1914 to 1921.

The building currently at 601 North Limestone.

A two-story building with the sign "Walker's Ice Cream and Confectionary" was part of a Lexington postcard collection. Research found that it was located at 601 North Limestone. "Hot Chili" was painted on the door. Research of the local newspapers shows that a big ice cream factory was established in Lexington in 1910 and 1914. Earlier, in October of 1908, The Lexington Ice Cream Company located on North Limestone was sold at public auction, and it belonged to the estate of the late W.T. Muir; but there was mention of Walker's Ice Cream and Confectionary.

The current Magnet School at 4th Street and North Limestone.

A postcard showing 601 North Limestone as Walker's Ice Cream and Confectionary. *On loan*.

The Lexington Senior High School is now a clothing and music store, located at 4th Street and North Limestone.

This Lexington Senior High School was located on the east side of North Limestone, at the corner of 4th Street, in 1918. It became a Lexington Traditional Magnet School. Other early High Schools include Henry Clay High School, opened in 1928, and Morton High School on Walnut Street. Henry Clay and Morton High Schools can be seen on old postcards in Chapter 8.

A postcard view identified as the Senior High School, Lexington, Kentucky. $.-5

The original building, the first of the Transylvania Medical School, was significant to the early history of Lexington. Local newspaper articles, one dated as March, 1822, reported that 36 diplomas were awarded to examined candidates at that time, and in 1826 the facilities were expanded to accommodate 500 students. The historic structure was demolished in March of 1954, to create a parking lot.

A postcard showing the last business at the northwest corner of Market and Church Streets. It was opened in 1823 as the first Transylvania Medical Hall. $3.-5

A current picture showing the northwest corner of Market and Church Streets.

The original building was opened in 1823 as the first Transylvania Medical Hall. It continued in that capacity for 30 years until the Hill Street Methodist Church purchased it for several years. In 1866 the building was sold to the city for a public library, a YMCA, and the University Club. The last business to occupy the building was the Hanson Magazine agency. This postcard shown was dated 1913, and inscribed, "We acknowledge with thanks the receipt of your remittance of $1.25 which will receive our immediate attention. Yours sincerely, J.M. Hanson, Lexington, Kentucky."

The corner of Walnut Street (currently known as Martin Luther King Boulevard) and Short Street is where the Central Christian Church was dedicated in 1894.

The current picture shows the corner of Martin Luther King Blvd. and Short Street as the location of the Central Christian Church.

An early postcard of the Central Christian Church, which was dedicated in 1894. *On loan.*

The corner of Martin Luther King Blvd. and Short street is where the Central Christian Church exists. City Hall was behind the church when this picture was made. When the City Hall location was photographed in the next picture, City Hall had been torn down.

The City Hall building was on Martin Luther King Boulevard, previously called Walnut Street. The pictured building is now part of the Central Christian Church facing on Short Street. City Hall offices were absorbed into the Urban County Government in the old Lafayette Hotel, now the Lexington City Government Building. Civil and Criminal Courts that were for years in the City Hall have been moved into two new buildings on Short and Limestone Streets. Their photos are shown in Chapter 8. The historian of this book, Harold Barker, started working for the city in this building in 1973. He worked in data processing department and moved into developing the Lexington Records and Archives department. By 1985, the collections had grown and were moved to the Lexington City Government building.

The previous location of the City Hall building near Short Street and the current Martin Luther King Boulevard.

An earlier view of City Hall was made before another façade was added in 1952. The corner stone for this building was laid in 1927.

This postcard shows an early view of the City Hall near Short and Walnut Streets $1-3

The Stop-Over-Station was located on the Esplanade and Short Street. It was used during World War II, with a kitchen and sleeping quarters for people in the Armed Forces. According to the *Lexington Herald*, the facility opened on February 28, 1942, and was supported entirely by local contributions. Any food, lodging, and other comforts were furnished to men or women in uniforms of U.S. or allied forces without cost. It closed January 31, 1946.

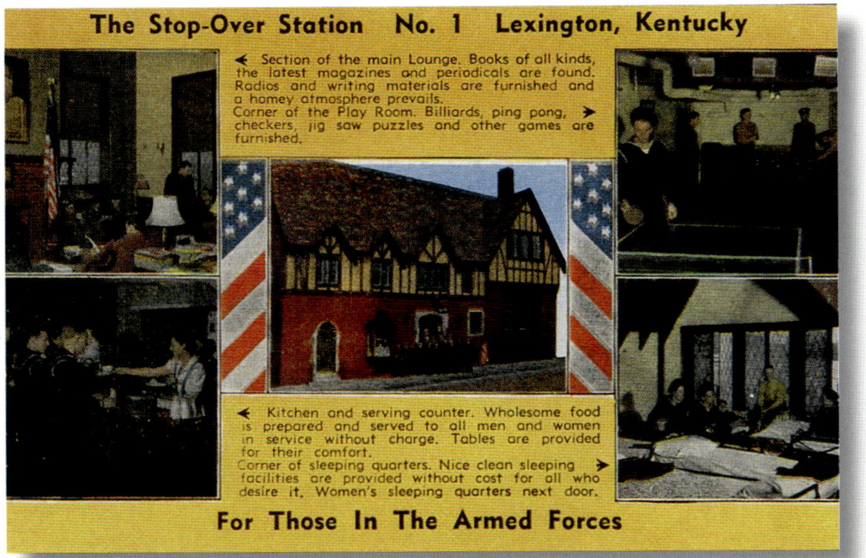

A postcard showing The-Stop-Over-Station located on the Esplanade and Short Street. *On loan*.

The current buildings at Esplanade and Short Street include the Chase Bank and a parking garage at 219 Short Street.

The first Good Samaritan Hospital started on East Short and Deweese Streets as the Protestant Infirmary in 1889; the name was changed in 1899. The old buildings now are used to store furniture for an office supply store. Good Samaritan Hospital moved to its current location on South Limestone and Maxwell Street in 1907. In 2007, the Good Samaritan Hospital sold its assets to the University of Kentucky and the building now is known as University of Kentucky Healthcare Good Samaritan Hospital.

Short and Deweese Streets with the current building.

The Good Samaritan Hospital had a glass domed operating room in a 3-story building in 1917.

A postcard of the Good Samaritan Hospital located at Short and DeWeese Streets. $1-3

A postcard of Morton High School on Walnut and Short Streets. *On loan*.

The Morton High School cornerstone was laid in 1909. The school was closed in 1939 and the building was demolished in 1940. Another view of this school can be seen in Chapter 8 in a postcard at the corner of E. Main and Walnut Streets.

The Chase Bank parking garage now occupies land that the former Morton High School had on the southeast corner of Walnut and Short Streets. Walnut Street has been renamed Martin Luther King Boulevard in more recent years.

The location of the old Morton High School, now a high-rise parking garage at Short Street and Martin Luther King Boulevard.

The old library is being used for literacy and learning. The newer library is shown in Chapter 8.

The old library that now is being used for other community purposes, at 251 West Second Street.

The Carnegie Library continued until the 1980s. As a new Public Library was built on East Main Street, this building became the Carnegie Center for Literacy and Learning.

This Carnegie Library was built in 1906. $1-3

On Mill and Second Streets, a well-known historical building is called Hopemont. The original owner, John W. Hunt, the first millionaire in the West, built the home in 1814. It has been operated as a museum since the mid-1900s.

Mill and Second Streets with a well-known, historical building called Hopemont or Hunt-Morgan Home

Hopemont, General Morgan's and John Hunt's home, has a porch and bay windows that were changed between 1891 and 1911.

The postcard shows Hopemont, the home of General Morgan and John Hunt. $1-3

A photo showing the front door of Hopemont.

Hopemont was a part of the Civil War conflict when General John Hunt Morgan achieved fame as "the greatest partisan raider in history." He grew up in his grandfather's home, Hopemont. The home remains a landmark in Lexington.

This postcard shows the front view of Hopemont, with members of the Hunt-Morgan family in a carriage. $3-5

Morrison Hall faced Third Street as a part of Transylvania University. A newer building is where the old Bible College building once stood.

This current picture shows Morrison Hall facing Third Street.

The old Bible College building facing toward North Broadway is on the left of this postcard.

A postcard shows Morrison Hall facing Third Street. $2-5

The current buildings at Fifth and Race Street are a federal housing project that occupied this site after the race course was dismantled in 1935.

The current buildings at Fifth and Race Streets.

The area around Fifth and Race Streets was a horse racing track named Kentucky Association. It had been in business since 1826; the original Race Track was cut up into town lots in 1899. A new stand was built and racing continued at the track until the spring of 1933.

Currently, Fifth and Race Streets has newer housing.

The current Fifth and Race Street location.

A postcard showing the area around Fifth and Race Streets when it was a race track. $2-5

A postcard view of the Fifth and Race Street race track. $1-3

The intersection of Bryan Station Pike and Paris Pike was the location of an earlier elementary school, where John Malick, the photographer for this book, was a student as a child

The current Bryan Station High School.

An early postcard shows Bryan Station High School between Bryan Station Pike and Paris Pike. *On loan.*

After years of being a horse farm, the owners promised a beautiful shopping mall for the site in October of 1999. By 2005, Hamburg Place received recognition for it's landscape and businesses within the complex.

Hamburg Place was a famous stock farm, having been established in 1898 by John E. Madden. This gateway was the entrance to a polo field. There were many local articles written about Hamburg Place, the earliest being on February, 1903, when John E. Madden added 348 acres to his adjoining stock farm on Winchester Road. In July of 1909, there were 103 thoroughbred brood mares in service at Hamburg Place, and by January of 1940, Hamburg Place had become a thoroughbred horse haven, in the role of steeplechasing. It was the home of at least five Kentucky Derby winners.

The current entrance to Hamburg Place.

A postcard view of the entrance to Hamburg Place. *On loan*.

Joyland Park was on Paris Pike. A bowling alley now stands where the old Joyland Amusement Park was located. It was a 25-acre amusement park two miles north of Lexington Street on Paris Pike. It opened in 1923 and closed around 1960 to 1963.

A view of Joyland Park at Paris Pike.

The current Hamburg Place shopping center.

An early postcard of Hamburg Place as a horse farm shows grass seed being delivered.

Hamburg Place as a horse farm. *On loan*.

Joyland Park became the recreation and amusement spot for Lexington during the second and third quarters of the 1900s.

A postcard showing the Dance Casino at Joyland Park. *On loan*.

A postcard view of Tony Martin, whose music was played at Joyland Park. *On loan*.

A housing subdivision now occupies the site where the Joyland Park existed.

Another view of the Joyland Park location.

A postcard shows Tony Martin, the popular singer and star of radio, stage, and screen, whose music was played at Joyland Park. This postcard was hand-signed by Tony Martin.

CHAPTER THREE
NORTH-WEST LEXINGTON

West of North Broadway and North of West Main Street

The former Independent Odd Fellows home, at 511 West Sixth Street, is now a housing complex.

The current 511 West Sixth Street

The Odd Fellows Orphans' Home was established in 1898 by the Independent Order of Odd Fellows. Early local newspaper articles report that the Odd Fellows and Orphans' Home was opened by members of the order. In 1909, a new Administration Building was added to the Odd Fellows' Widows' and Orphans' Home. Two four-story buildings were part of a 68-acre farm and accommodated 200 orphaned children, who were cared for until they were old enough to support themselves. A newspaper article dated June 10, 1940, reported that nearly 800 people attended the annual homecoming and visitation day at the I.O.O.F. Children's home on West Sixth Street.

The Independent Order of Odd Fellows Home. *On loan.*

Hampton Court is on West Third Street, between Jefferson Street and North Broadway. There have been no major changes to the residential subdivision except that the trees have grown.

The Hampton Court on West Third Street between Jefferson and North Broadway.

For many years, a two-story brick building stood on West Third Street known as the Lexington Orphan Asylum at the entrance of Hampton Court. It is not visible on this postcard. Today Hampton Court is a residential subdivision.

This postcard shows the entrance to Hampton Court. *On loan*.

At 544 W. Second Street, the previous St. Joseph Hospital is now the site of city-supported apartments for the elderly.

544 W. Second Street, previously the St. Joseph Hospital.

A 1910 postcard shows the first location of St. Joseph Hospital. The hospital was founded in 1877 at 320 Linden Walk, and was relocated to 544 West Second Street in 1878. This building was added in 1906. Notice the old cars.

The first location of the St. Joseph Hospital, 1910. $3-5

The St. Joseph Hospital building was abandoned in 1959 and razed in 1966. The new St. Joseph Hospital moved to the corner of Waller Avenue and Harrodsburg Road.

A current view of 544 W. Second Street, taken from across the street.

A postcard view of the St. Joseph Hospital at 544 W. Second Street. $2-3

Location of Euphrasia Hall at 544 West Second Street, the nurses' residence.

Euphrasia Hall of the St.Joseph Hospital was a nurses' residence at 523 W. Second Street. It was connected to the hospital by an underground tunnel. The buildings were torn down in 1966, and Harold Barker, a consultant for this book, reports that the tunnel is still there and future plans include exploring it.

A postcard view of Euphrasia Hall. $1-2

Eastern State Hospital on West Fourth Street, as it is today.

Eastern State Hospital, on West Fourth Street, was opened as a Lunatic Asylum in 1824; it continues as a mental hospital today and there are plans to replace it. The author worked as a psychologist here from 1967 to 1996, while observing and documenting its many changes.

The right front building was the original Lunatic Asylum. The Administration building on the left was added in 1894. Eastern State Hospital has a long history of following American psychiatric trends.

A postcard of the Eastern State Hospital. $6-7

The current building at Eastern State Hospital was built in 1868 and is now empty, while treatment of the mentally ill has shifted to community care. The building was connected to an infirmary that was added in 1899. That infirmary was mentioned in the September 7, 1914, local newspaper as a "Modern Sanitarium" for the open-air treatment of tuberculosis. It was built to accommodate 30 patients. At that time, the insane were the only ones to receive treatment for this disease in Fayette County, but changes came the next year. A new Tuberculosis Sanitarium was opened for local citizens.

It is important to recognize that the history of Eastern State Hospital is symbolic of not only psychiatric but also medical history in Kentucky.

The name Eastern Kentucky Asylum for the Insane was used from 1876 to 1894, and was one of fourteen names for Eastern State Hospital. The postcard shown was published in 1910, but the picture was made around 1900 before the administration building was joined to the 1868 building. An old ballroom on the top floor of the administration building, once part of Lexington's social fabric, is now vacant. A wooden Christmas manger scene is visible between the buildings, showing that this picture was made in early December when Christmas decorations were throughout the grounds.

The author has an extensive collection of Lunatic Asylum postcards, including those of Eastern State Hospital. Until 1915, most asylums were highly regarded and the postcards often reflected that pride. After 1915, social attitudes declined towards the asylums and their successors, the state mental hospitals.

This postcard identifies The Eastern Kentucky Asylum for the Insane, Lexington. $5-7

Eastern State Hospital.

The former Julius Marks Tuberculosis Sanatorium/Sanitarium on Georgetown Street is now a new Church of God building.

The Tuberculosis Sanitarium was located here.

This postcard view shows the treatment facility of the period, a Tuberculosis Sanitarium. $2-5

A 1950s postcard identifies a treatment facility of the period, called Tuberculosis Sanitarium. It was later identified by the City Directory as the Julius Marks Tuberculosis Sanatorium. This facility was identified on a 1947 map as a Sanatorium, and on a 1986 map as the Blue Grass Sanitarium, all located on U.S. 25 and/or Georgetown Street. Local newspaper articles, on March 2, 1915, reported that the City appropriated $2,500 for a tuberculosis sanitarium, while levy taxes were raised for a Sanitarium. This one opened in 1917 and the main building was named for Dr. McDowell, who advanced and practiced a modern cure for tuberculosis.

The previous location of Campbell-Hagerman College was at 437 West Second Street. The current apartment building is in private ownership.

Professor Hagerman purchased a large house at 437 W. Second Street to establish a college in 1903. It had a faculty of twelve and awarded A.B. degrees. 150 women were enrolled in 1906 and nearly 200 young ladies graduated from this college before it closed in 1912. One local article stated that the college was one of the leading female educational institutions in the South.

The current remains of the Campbell-Hagerman College, at 437 West Second Street.

A postcard shows the Campbell-Hagerman College. *On loan*.

Meadowthorpe Shopping area is located on West Main Street at Forbes Road.

The current Meadowthorpe Shopping area.

Local newspaper articles reported the Meadowthorpe Farm in 1892 consisting of 222 acres. It was sold in 1907 from the estate of Col. JamesE. Pepper as the very best tract of Blue Grass land. Lexington's first airport as on Boling Springs Drive part of the Meadowthorpe land, called Halley Field. This was where Charles A. Lindbergh made an overnight stop in March of 1928. A subdivision was developed from the former Meadowthorpe stock farm in 1949.

A postcard showing a residence on the Meadowthorpe Stock Farm. *On loan*.

Edw. R. Bradley, owner of Idle Hour Farm on old Frankfort Pike, died in 1946. The Galbreath family purchased the property and renamed it Darby Dan Farm.

Darby Dan Farm was previously part of the Idle Hour Farm.

A current photograph of the entrance to Darby Dan Farm.

Postcard of Idle Hour Farm. *On loan.*

In the 1940s, Idle Hour Farm had a race track.

Current photo of Darby Dan Farm.

Aerial view of Idle Hour Farm. *On loan.*

CHAPTER FOUR

SOUTH LEXINGTON

On South Broadway towards U.S. Highway 68 South

The west side of South Broadway at Vine Street is currently a shopping mall, with a hotel and park in the center of the old town. Water Street was combined with Vine Street years earlier.

The Lexington Roller Mills Company opened in 1884 on Water and Vine Streets. It manufactured flour, meal, and feed that created such brands as Lexington Cream, Henry Clay Flour, Hoe Cake Meal, and Thoroughbred Feed. This postcard was published from 1907 to 1915. Notice that the building was three stories on the front.

The current west side of South Broadway at Water and Vine Streets.

The Lexington Roller Mills Company on Water and Vine Streets. $2-5.

Another view of South Broadway and Vine Street shows a bank, hotel, shopping mall, and park across the street from where the Lexington Roller Mills existed.

The corner of South Broadway and Water Street.

The Lexington Roller Mills existed at this location as early as 1884, when a local newspaper article stated that it received daily installments of 350,000 bushels of wheat, for which they paid $.75 per bushel. An article of January 10, 1904, confirmed the opening date of 1884 and the success from able management. The plant originally started with a two hundred barrel capacity per day, and has steadily increased to 500 barrels. This postcard is of the linen era, therefore it was a view around the 1950s and the mill was then five stories high. The building was demolished in 1968.

A view of the Lexington Roller Mills, Inc. *On loan.*

The location of 701 South Broadway is where old railroad tracks still exist.

The current scene at 701 South Broadway.

A two-story, yellow brick building was at the corner of 701 South Broadway. It was built in 1908 and later became the Southern Railroad Depot. The postcard was printed by Wrenn and King, located at the corner of West Main and Mill Streets.

South Broadway today is the former location of tobacco warehouses.

A depot at the corner of Broadway and Angliana Avenue, or 701 South Broadway. The publisher was Wrenn and King. $3-5.

South Broadway as it appears today.

South Broadway was lined with tobacco wagons headed for the market. The tobacco warehouses were mostly located on Angliana Avenue, Bolivar, and South Upper Streets. A city directory of Lexington in 1910-1911 identified three tobacco warehouses on South Broadway, but by 1919 the number had grown to ten.

South Broadway was lined with tobacco wagons headed for the market. *On loan*.

St. Joseph Hospital was at Waller Avenue and Harrodsburg Pike.

St. Joseph's Hospital at Waller Avenue and Harrodsburg Pike.

High Oaks and Dr. Sprague's Sanatorium became the final residence for wealthy citizens such as Charlton Hunt Morgan, who died there at the age of 74. An article dated July 25, 1912, stated that Dr. Sprague, proprietor of High Oaks, would move his Sanatorium from South Broadway to Harrodsburg Pike when new buildings were complete. It later became a prominent hospital for local citizens and was demolished in 1958.

Another view of the St. Joseph Hospital.

High Oaks Sanatorium stood on fourteen acres at the corner of Waller Avenue and Harrodsburg Pike. A local newspaper article of January 1,1892 states that Dr. Silas Evans purchased the High Oaks Sanatorium property on South Broadway from his father-in-law, Dr. R.C. Chenault. Within the next ten years, Dr. Sprague was the owner, and it was a private facility associated with the treatment of tuberculosis.

This postcard shows the location of the High Oaks Sanatorium at the corner of Waller Avenue and Harrodsburg Pike. $8-15 as a whole postcard.

A part of the 1910 postcard of High Oaks and Dr. Sprague's Sanatorium. $8-15 as a whole postcard.

In the 1950s, the tack room at the Campbell house was listed on U.S. Highway 68, before the city limits grew out to the area.

A postcard shows the tack room at the Campbell house. *On loan*.

The Campbell House on South Broadway opened July 23, 1951. In 1976, the Campbell House celebrated twenty-five years of successful growth. New owners renovated the facility in 2003, changing its interior 370 rooms.

The current Campbell House on South Broadway.

The Springs Motel on South Broadway was within the city of Lexington.

The current Springs Motel.

The current Springs Motel has rooms on two levels.

The current Springs Motel

A postcard view of the Springs Motel. $1-3

The Springs Motel, between 1930 and 1940, claimed to accommodate 182 people. It was located a mile south of Lexington on Highway 68. The rooms were on one level with a two-story building in the middle.

A postcard that shows the Springs Motel. It still accommodated 182 people on one level located on Highway 68.

A postcard showing the Springs Motel. $1.50-3.

A postcard of the Springs Motel in 1968 claimed it to have 114 units, with a heated swimming pool and free television. It was located at 2020 South Broadway.

This postcard of the Springs Motel was sent in 1968. $2-4

The Springs Motel has two levels of rooms and is located within the city of Lexington.

Another current picture of the Springs Motel.

CHAPTER FIVE

SOUTH-EAST LEXINGTON

East of South Broadway and South of East Main Street

The 400 East Vine Street building has small offices and shops.

The 400 East Vine Street office building as it appears today.

The Taylor Tire Company opened on November 15, 1930. It had moved from 342 E. Main Street with the state's most modern tire establishment and home of the Seiberling tires. In 1923, when the old "tin lizzie" was still a popular means of travel, J.S. Taylor started his business. He was one of twenty independent tire dealers locally, and after a quarter of a century, he was the only one still doing business in 1950. The business closed in 1980.

A postcard view of the Taylor Tire Company. *On loan.*

The Lexington Theological Seminary was previously called The College of the Bible, and is now located on South Limestone Street.

The current Lexington Theological Seminary

The University of Kentucky now is located on several streets, including South Limestone and Euclid Avenue, or Avenue of Champions.

The University of Kentucky off South Broadway, front view.

An aerial view shows The College of the Bible from a 1960s postcard.

A postcard showing the College of Bible. $1-3

Between 1907 and 1915, a parcel of land was preserved for the University of Kentucky.

This postcard was produced between 1907 and 1915 showing the University of Kentucky. $2-5

The old Administration Building and newer buildings are identified with the University of Kentucky on South Limestone.

In 1907, the Administration Building of Kentucky State College was located on South Limestone Street. A map of Lexington in 1903 listed Kentucky University at North Broadway, between Third and Fourth Streets, which later became Transylvania University. Kentucky State College listed on South Limestone later became the University of Kentucky.

This postcard shows the Administration Building of Kentucky State College on South Broadway. $2-5

A current picture of the old Administration Building on South Broadway.

The old University of Kentucky Administration Building had a fire and required some remodeling.

A left view of the old Administration Building.

In 1919, the Administration Building was part of the State University.

This postcard shows the same building as part of the State University. $1-3

The Agricultural Experiment Station is now part of the University of Kentucky.

A current photograph shows the Experiment Station Building.

The Agricultural Experiment Station was identified as the A & M College, in 1909. A & M stood for Agricultural and Mechanical College, established in 1866 in Lexington. It moved to its present location in 1882.

A postcard view of the New Experiment Station is identified as the A & M College. $4-6

Patterson Hall is at the University of Kentucky.

Patterson Hall was part of the Kentucky State College in 1908.

Patterson Hall as it appears today.

A current picture of Patterson Hall.

This postcard shows Patterson Hall when it was part of State College. $1-3

Patterson Hall in 1942 was known as the University of Kentucky women's dormitory.

This postcard shows Patterson Hall when it was part of the University of Kentucky. 1.50-3

Memorial Hall is one of the most photographed buildings on the University of Kentucky campus.

Memorial Hall was dedicated in 1929 to Kentuckians who died in World War I.

A current picture of Memorial Hall.

A 1950s postcard showing Memorial Hall. $1-3

The current University of Kentucky's Medical School was created within the University of Kentucky.

In 1935, an air view shows the University of Kentucky, prior to the Medical School being added.

A view of the University of Kentucky Medical School.

A 1935 postcard view of the University of Kentucky. $1-3

The University of Kentucky now has a College of Business and Economics building.

A view of the University of Kentucky.

A 1956 air view of the University of Kentucky shows three small buildings on the right side of Memorial Hall prior to the College of Business and Economics building.

The Otis Singletary Center, on Rose and Euclid Streets, replaced the old Stadium.

A more recent aerial postcard of University of Kentucky. $1-3

A postcard view of the Stadium and Coliseum. *On loan.*

The University of Kentucky's old football stadium has been replaced, but The Coliseum remains the same outside.

The current University of Kentucky Commonwealth Stadium is located at Alumni Drive and South Limestone Street.

The Coliseum on Euclid Avenue was built in 1950 and was dedicated to World War II soldiers. It replaced the Alumni Gym, which had been built at another location on Euclid Avenue.

A 1965 view of the Coliseum. $.50-2

Aylesford Place, between Maxwell Street and Rose Lane near the campus of University of Kentucky, has rental apartments.

A current view of Aylesford Place.

Aylesford Place was a residential street. The subdivision was built in 1919.

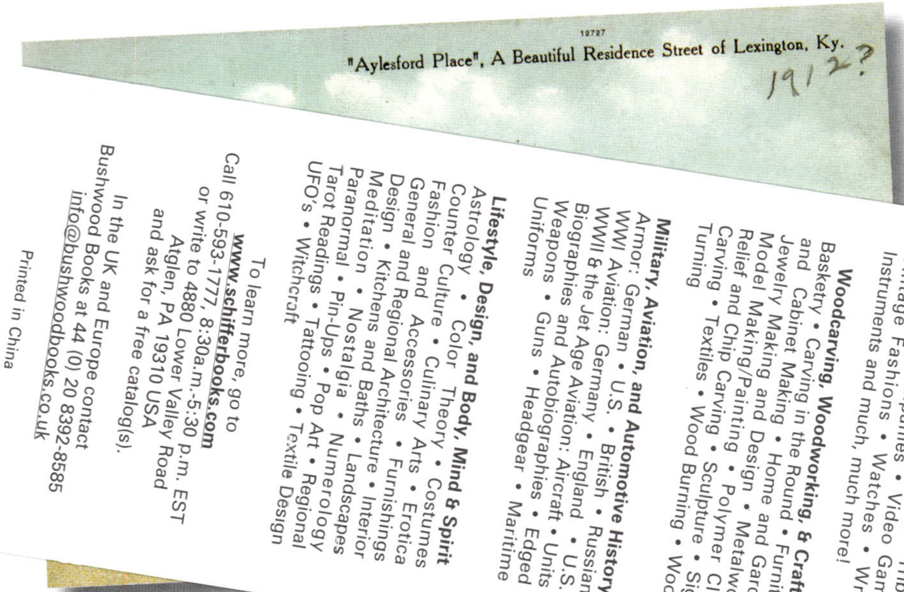

A postcard view of Aylesford Place. $2-4

The Good Samaritan Hospital is on South Limestone Street.

…ood Samaritan Hospital.

In 1948, the Ott Building at the Good Samaritan Hospital was on South Limestone Street.

A postcard view of the Ott Building at the Good Samaritan Hospital on South Limestone. $.50-3

A 35-unit hotel at the site of the old Yocum's Motor Lodge was started in 1997 at 1229 S. Limestone Street.

The current view of 1229 South Limestone.

The current Central Baptist Hospital is located at 1740 South Limestone Street.

The current Central Baptist Hospital

Yocum's Lodge at 1229 South Limestone. $3-5

Yocum's Lodge, at 1229 S. Limestone Street, was torn down in 1988, following the killing of a customer the previous year.

Central Baptist Hospital was built in 1954 at 1740 South Limestone Street.

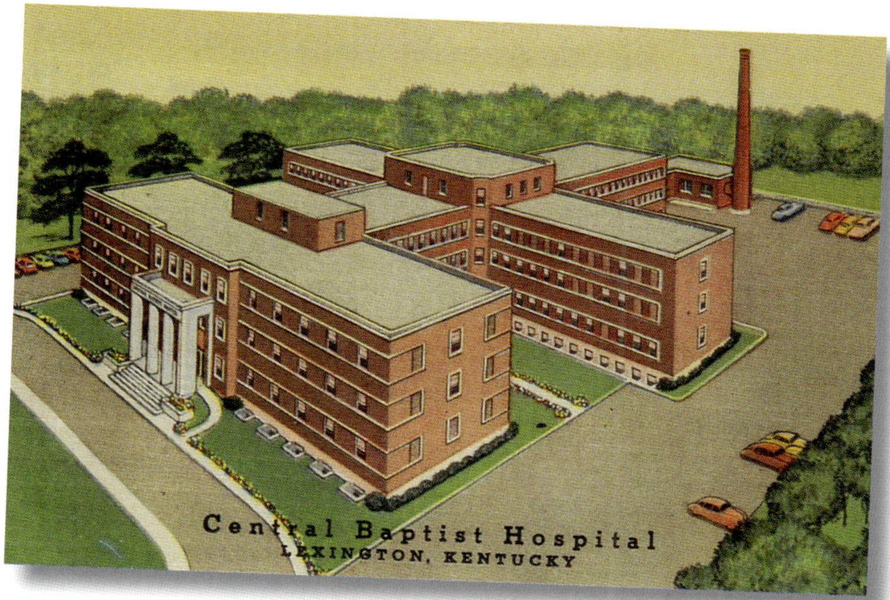

An early view of Central Baptist Hospital. *On loan*.

Another view of Central Baptist Hospital. $.50-3

A 1970s view of Central Baptist Hospital.

The northeast corner of Kentucky Avenue and High Street features Woodland Park.

A current picture of the northeast corner at Kentucky Ave. and East High Street.

An earlier wooden auditorium was replaced by a brick auditorium in 1906 in Woodland Park. The Auditorium was demolished in 1941.

A postcard showing the brick auditorium located in Woodland Park. *On loan*.

Woodland Park is a popular retreat at the corner of Kentucky Avenue and High Street.

A current picture of Kentucky Avenue and East High Street.

One of the productions at the Woodland Auditorium Theatre on March 17th, titled *Faversham's Triumph* by Stephen Phillip, was advertised on this 1920s postcard. It quoted *The Lexington Herald*, New York critics, and other newspapers claiming this play as "A feast for the eye and a joy to the ear."

The Woodland Park Association was organized in 1882 and purchased 110 acres in the east side of town. A 1910 view of Woodland Park shows it to have been a major park at that time.

One of the productions at the Woodland Park Auditorium Theatre, on March 17th, titled *Faversham's Triumph* by Stephen Phillip, was advertised on this postcard. *On loan*. $2-5

This postcard shows a view of Woodland Park. $2-5

Woodland has a bandstand at Kentucky Avenue and High Street.

A current picture taken at Kentucky Avenue and East High Street, the location of the Auditorium in Woodland Park.

CHAPTER SIX
SOUTH-WEST LEXINGTON

West of South Broadway and South of West Main Street

The Red Mile Trotting Track is between South Broadway and Versailles Road.

A current photograph of The Red Mile Trotting Track.

The Kentucky Trotting Breeders Association's stockholders acquired this property in 1892 from the old Kentucky Agricultural & Mechanical Society. This postcard of the grandstand was sent in 1910.

A postcard view of the early grandstands at the Kentucky Trotting Breeders Association. $5-8

The Red Mile Trotting Track entrance has seen several changes that have been reflected in local newspaper articles, such as one of September 21, 1973, that stated that "the Red Mile Centennial publication had been completed by Lexingtonians who were devoted to the sport." Another article related that the Red Mile Clubhouse got some new décor and a manager in 1975. A still later article told how a new look for the Red Mile has added for 46 nights of harness racing in 1986. On September 25, 2000, the trotting track was attempting a rebirth in the racing community, as new owners had spent $4 million on renovations.

A current photograph of The Red Mile Trotting Track.

The grandstands of the Kentucky Trotting Tracks replaced the previous ones burned in 1931. These were built of steel and concrete.

A postcard view of the Red Mile Trotting Track grandstands, which were built with steel and concrete, $2-.

A postcard shows the Yearling Sales at the Keeneland Race Track. $1-2

The Hawkins Funeral Home is at West Pine and Merino Streets.

The John T. Hawkins Funeral Home was built in 1936 at 632 Pine Street. Mrs. Ann Hawkins Taylor, owner and licensed embalmer, began operating the funeral home in 1947, after John Hawkins died. She continued until her death in 1984.

A current picture of Pine and Merino Streets.

A postcard view of the John T. Hawkins Funeral Home. *On loan*.

The Keeneland Race Track was located on Versailles Road.

The current view of Keeneland Race Track, located on Versailles Road.

The Keeneland Association Running Track was pictured in a postcard mailed in 1942. The Kentucky Association Race track had been at Fifth and Race Streets until 1933 when the track and grandstand were dismantled in 1935. Pictures of the earlier track are seen in Chapter 2.

A postcard, mailed in 1942, shows the Keeneland Association Running Track. $1-3

The current Keeneland Race Track remains a fixture in Lexington.

A current picture shows the Keeneland Race Track entrance.

Current views of the Blue Grass Airport are prohibited. A distant view of an Eastern Airlines plane at the Blue Grass Airport was taken from an old postcard.

A postcard view of an Eastern Airlines plane at the Blue Grass Airport. $3-4

A closer view of the Blue Grass Airport from another postcard shows that Delta and Eastern were the first commercial airlines out of the airport after 1946. Previously, it served as a runway during World War II.

A postcard view of the Blue Grass Airport. $1-2

A current photo of U.S. Highway 60 at the western City Limits shows the Day's Motel.

A recent photograph of U.S. Highway 60, at the western city limits.

Day's Motel served Lexington visitors from 1930 to 2007. It was owned and operated by Mr. & Mrs. J.B. Day from 1930 to 1945. It had 35 rooms and was located in the center of Kentucky's horse-breeding and racing country on U.S. Highway 60.

A postcard view of Day's Motel, about 1930 to 1945. *On loan*.

This Day's Motel postcard was mailed in 1952 when it was operated by J.B. Day and his son. The motel at that time had 54 rooms and was part of the United Motor Courts and AAA.

A postcard view of Day's Motel that was mailed in 1952. $4-5

A recent photograph of Day's Motel, on U.S. Highway 60, at the western city limits.

CHAPTER SEVEN
WEST LEXINGTON
On West Main towards the center of town to Limestone Street

Spindletop Stock Farm as it is today.

A 1950s postcard of the Spindletop Stock Farm shows an 800-acre farm on Iron Works Pike, on the West side of town, that was established in 1935. The farm was given to the University of Kentucky in 1959 to be used as an Alumni-Faculty Club.

A current view of the Spindletop Stock Farm

A 1950s postcard view of the Spindletop Stock Farm. $1-2

The entrance to the Federal Prison is located on Leestown Pike. Pictures inside the facility are prohibited.

The current view of a federal prison on Leestown Pike.

The Veterans' Hospital on Leestown Pike.

A postcard view of the U.S. Public Health Farm, located on Leestown Pike. $.50-2.

The U.S. Public Health Farm was located on Leestown Pike before it became a Federal Prison.

The Veterans' Hospital, claiming to be one of the most modern institutions of its kind, opened in May, 1931.

An early postcard view of the Veterans' Hospital. $1-2

Lexington Cemetery was founded in 1849 on West Main Street.

An early postcard view shows the Chapel and Henry Clay Monument at the Lexington Cemetery. *On loan*.

The Cemetery Chapel, with Henry Clay's Monument on the right, is in the Lexington Cemetery. The original Romanesque Revival Style building was replaced by a gatehouse in 1890.

The current entrance to the Lexington Cemetery.

Lexington Cemetery is located on West Main Street.

The lake in Lexington Cemetery.

The Henry Clay Monument in the Lexington Cemetery is a local attraction that was completed on July 4, 1861.

A current view of The Henry Clay Monument in Lexington Cemetery.

The Henry Clay Monument on a postcard sent in 1907. $2-3

An August 22, 1990, newspaper article reporteded that the Lexington Cemetery is a 170-acre oasis of trees and flowers just on the outskirts of downtown. It is on the National Register of Historic Places and has gained a national reputation as an arboretum with more than 200 species of trees.

A postcard shows the lake in the Lexington Cemetery. $2-3

The extension of the Jefferson Street Viaduct goes north and south from West Main Street.

The Jefferson Street Viaduct as it is today.

The West Main Street Viaduct is still there. An article about this Viaduct occurred in a July 23, 1905, newspaper, stating that the establishment of a viaduct through Ayers Alley from Main to High Street "has produced strong public sentiment as it facilitated traffic."

The West Main Street Viaduct as it appeared in the early 1900s. $2-4

224 West Main Street is on the south side and across from the old Court House.

224 West Main Street as it appears today.

The Colonial Theatre is located at 224 West Main Street. By 1906, six movie theaters had opened in Lexington. The Colonial was the most beautiful and up-to-date motion picture theater in central Kentucky. The manager of it that year was J.B. Elliott.

A postcard showing the Colonial Theatre. *On loan.*

This outside view of the Ross Shipp Company Department Store is at 216 W. Main St., prior to the name change in 1913. A newspaper article of September 28, 1913, reported that the Ross-Shipp store had a new front and was incorporated as the Ross-Shipp Company.

An outside view shows the Ross Shipp Co. department store at 216 West Main Street. *On loan.*

The current scene at 216 West Main Street.

An inside view shows the ready-to-wear department at the Ross Shipp Company store at 216 West Main Street. $5-6

Postcard view of West Main Street from Broadway to Upper Street around the 1920s.

A postcard view shows West Main Street from Broadway to Upper Street. $2-4

West Main Street as it appears from Broadway towards Upper Street.

Mill Street includes a southeast corner advertisement for E.B.Wrenn Wallpaper and Postcards. Many Lexington postcard views were produced by Wrenn & King, including a postcard by Judge James H. Mulligan, in Kentucky, in 1907. A newspaper article of January 1, 1917, reported that negotiations were made between E.B. King & Co. (books, stationary and job printer) and E.B. Wrenn, a wall paper, picture frames & novelties seller. In 1934, E.B. Wrenn died at the age of 79 at his home on Sycamore Road.

The current view of West Main Street from the corner of Mill Street towards Upper Street.

A postcard view shows the corner of Mill Street from West Main Street to Upper Street. $5-6

Another view of West Main Street towards Upper Street.

Another postcard view from Mill Street on West Main Street towards Upper Street. While the bank building on the left remains the same, the building on the corner of Upper Street was later replaced by the New Fayette Bank Building.

The First and City National Bank, on West Main and Cheapside Streets, was created as First and City Bank in 1865 and became the First National Bank in 1919. That Bank merged in 1929 with the Phoenix Bank and assumed control of the Fayette National Bank in 1936 at Main and Upper Streets.

A postcard view from Mill Street on West Main Street towards Upper Street. $2-6

A current view of the building at the corner of West Main Street and Cheapside Streets.

A postcard of the First and City National Bank on West Main Street and Cheapside Streets. *On pa[illegible].*

A current photograph of the southwest corner of West Main and Mill Streets.

The Current view looking west, from the corner of West Main.

A postcard view looking west, down West Main Street. The J.D. Purcell Company is identified on the left. $1-3

The F.M. Kirby Ten Cent Store was located on the southwest corner of West Main and Mill Streets. This postcard was mailed in 1913. A newspaper article on July 23, 1908, reported the new store of F.M. Kirby & Co. as a large five-and-ten-cent store in the city, and a similar store was to be established in Frankfort, Kentucky.

The current view at the southwest corner of Main and Mill Streets, looking west on Main Street.

A postcard view of The F.M. Kirby Ten Cent Store that was located on the south-west corner of West Main and Mill Streets. $1-3

A postcard view of the southwest corner of Mill and Main Streets, looking toward West Main, $3-6

A newspaper article of November 8, 1904, stated that the J.D. Purcell Company moved to 326 West Main Street for its regular opening. It continued to operate as a downtown department store until January 1, 1970. The five-story building was on the south side of West Main, between Mill and Broadway, and the postcard was mailed in 1911.

Current view of West Main Street and Mill Street.

Postcard of J.D. Purcell Company. *On loan*.

West Main Street and Mill Street as they look today.

Postcard showing R. S. Thorpe and Sons, Clothing and Furnishing Store for men, located at West Main and Mill Streets.

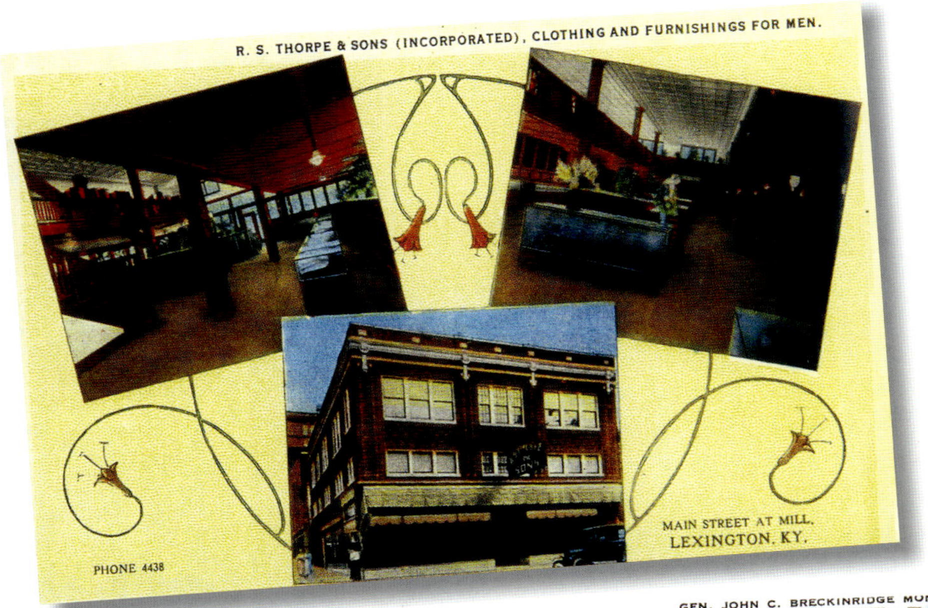

Postcard of R. S. Thorpe and Sons, at West Main and Mill Streets. *On loan*.

The John C. Breckinridge Monument is located in Cheapside Park. The statue was added on an anniversary of his flight to the Confederacy on September 9, 1887. He was a U.S. Senator from Kentucky, Vice President of U.S. under James Buchanan, Army General, and Secretary of War under the Confederacy.

A postcard of the John C. Breckinridge Monument located in Cheapside Park. *On loan*.

A current view of the John C. Breckinridge Monument located in Cheapside Park.

A current view of Main and Cheapside Streets around the Court House, taken from Short Street.

A current view of Cheapside Street around the Court House.

Another current view of Main and Cheapside Streets around the Court House.

Court Day was a monthly gathering in Lexington that was reported as early as 1893, with "Court Day Orators" and an unusually large crowd of farmers and country folk in town. Cheapside was full. By October 1, 1895, a decline in Court Day attendance was reported. With the building of stockyards in the county and the sale of cattle on the public square becoming prohibited, the death knell of this enjoyable gathering was at hand. Yet, on July 1, 1984, an article stated that a recent Court Day had lured 5,000 people downtown. Instead of the overpowering stench of manure on earlier Court Days, then there was the smell of apple pies, popcorn, hot dogs, and sandwiches in downtown Lexington.

A postcard view of a Court Day Scene around the Court House. $1-6

Another current view of Main and Cheapside Streets around the Court House taken from Main Street.

A front view of Court Day Scene around Cheapside Street and the Breckinridge Monument. In a newspapter article of April 21, 1830, reported a show of brood horses at the April Court Day drawing a large crowd with 35 horses. Notice the people around what was then, the trolley car station.

A front view of the Court Day Scene around the Breckinridge Monument. $6-12

Day view of Court House. Current location of the Lexington History Museum.

A day view of the old Court House

A day view of the Court House with trolley cars, $1-3

A postcard of the old City National Bank building, and the old Court House.

Current photo of Old Court House and Upper Street. It is the location of The Lexington History Museum.

A current picture of the Court House and The Fayette National Bank.

A postcard showing the center of town with the City National Bank, Old Court House, and the New Fayette National Bank. This postcard was sent in 1926.

The center of town is pictured with the City National Bank, Court House, and the New Fayette National Bank on this postcard, which was sent in 1926. $1-3

The current Court House and Upper Street.

A closer view of the Court House and Upper Street. It is the current location of the Lexington History Museum.

A postcard of the Court House, The Fayette Bank Building and the Star Theatre on Upper Street. The postcard was sent in 1928.

A postcard that was sent in 1928, of the Court House, The Fayette Bank building, and the Star Theatre around Upper Street. $1-3

A current picture of what was the Fayette Bank Building on Upper Street. On April 27, 1931, the First National Bank assumed control of the Fayette National Bank and moved into its fifteen story building.

A current picture of the First National Bank building.

Another postcard of the Court House and The Fayette Bank Building on Upper Street. The postcard was sent in 1942.

A postcard showing the Court House and The Fayette Bank building on Upper Street. It was mailed in 1942. $1-3

The new Fayette National Bank Building postcard sent in 1914. A Fayette National Bank was erected in 1913-14 on the northeast corner of Main and Upper Streets. A previous three story-brick Fayette National Bank was erected in 1871-72 and was razed for this newer structure. In the 1919 City Directory, this Fayette National Bank Building had many offices occupied throughout the building. One, the Law Office of Allen and Duncan #1504, were researched and written about in the book, "The Early Gatekeepers", 2005, written by Deese. These two partners reflect years of long family ties and service to the City of Lexington.

This postcard of the new Fayette National Bank Building was mailed in 1914. $1-3

Current picture of old Court House which is now a local history museum.

A current picture of the old Court House, which is now a local history museum.

A 1905 postcard of the Court House and first skyscraper, the McClellan Building on the right and the Northern Bank Building on the left.

An early postcard showing the Court House and first sky-scraper, the McClellan Building, on the right and the Northern Bank Building on the left, published by the Roto-graph Co. and copy-righted in 1905. $3-6

Current picture of the General John H. Morgan Monument on the east side of the old Court House.

A 1912 postcard of the General John H. Morgan Monument on the east side of the Court House. The statue was unveiled in October 1911. He was raised in Lexington, fought in the Confederate Army, and was killed by a Union Soldier on Sept. 4, 1864 in Tennessee. Notice the Star Theatre in the background, which opened in 1907.

A current picture of the General John H. Morgan Monument on the east side of the old Court House.

A postcard, showing the General John H. Morgan Monument on the east side of the Court House, was sent in 1912. $4-6

CHAPTER EIGHT

EAST LEXINGTON

From Limestone Street on East Main toward Richmond Road

A distant photograph taken from the corner of Limestone Street looks west, down East Main Street to the Old Court House, and on to the current location of The Lexington History Museum.

A postcard of East Main Street shows the area from Limestone Street towards the old Court House. Notice the building with the E.C. Kidd advertising on the north side of the building.

A photograph of Main Street, looking from the corner of Limestone Street towards the Court House.

A postcard showing Main Street between the Court House and Limestone Street. It was published for F.W. Woolworth Co. $1-6

A closer photo features the area from Limestone Street west towards the old Court House and the current location of The Lexington History Museum.

An early postcard of East Main Street taken from Limestone Street. The E.C. Kidd advertising and an arcade are visible on the right, while the Leonard Hotel and Graves Cox Company is on the left. The postcard was sent in 1913.

A current photograph shows Main Street, between Upper and Limestone Streets.

A postcard view of Main Street, between Upper and Limestone Streets, sent in 1913. $3-8

At the 100 block of East Main Street, the old buildings of that block all have been torn down for newer construction.

A current view of 134 East Main Street.

A postcard showing the United Clothing Stores for men and boys at 134 East Main Street was issued in the 1920s. An article dated Sept 21, 1912, stated that J.B.Calvert of Harrodsburg, representing the United Clothing Company which had a store in Mercer County, was leasing a vacant store in Lexington.

A postcard of the United Clothing Stores for men and boys. *On loan*.

A current picture of East Main Street from Martin Luther King Blvd.

The Phoenix Hotel is shown on the left with an eagle on the top. It had been on the south side of Main and Limestone since 1797, and was razed in the 1980s.

A postcard showing East Main Street, from Walnut Street looking west. $4-8

Another postcard of East Main Street includes the Phoenix Hotel on the left. It was sent in 1914.

This postcard shows East Main Street, with the Phoenix Hotel on the left. It was mailed December 20, 1914, and is inscribed , "Dear home folks. We mailed the Xmas box and will rite yu all a letter soon. We are both well and hardy. Mr. M. weights his ---- 200 lbs xmas day. Hope all are well, Ella." $2-8

East Main Street now has buildings facing Upper Street that include the Civil and Criminal Court Buildings.

A current photograph of East Main Street, near Martin Luther King Boulevard.

Military marching on East Main Street during World War II was part of the war effort by members of the Red Cross. A Stop-over Station for soldiers was opened on Feb. 28, 1942, at 109 Esplanade Street. It closed on January 31, 1946.

Military men marching on East Main Street, before Walnut Street, during World War II. *On loan.*

A newspaper article of Sept. 30, 1923, stated that the department store Wolf Wile Company would open October 1, 1923, next door to the Hernando Building. On June 21, 1982, Joseph Sable Wile, 76, had worked in his family's business at Wolf Wile for 55 years. The store had two locations, 322-324 West Main Street and 244 East Main Street. It closed on April 4, 1992, after 103 years; and Joseph S. Wile, Sr. retired at the age of 86.

A view on the south side of East Main Street, next to where the Union Train Station and Viaduct stood.

A postcard view of the Wolf Wile Company, Central Kentucky's great department store, which was next to the Union Train Station, Viaduct, and buildings on the south side. *On loan*.

The Golden Horseshoe Restaurant and Cocktail Lounge was located at 124 East Main Street. It existed from 1948 to 1960, with Ralph B. and Mabel Campbell as owners. A newspaper article of February 1, 1950, stated that Ralph B. Campbell, owner of the Golden Horseshoe, had asked a city-county planning commission to build a new hotel on land he owned at the intersection of Harrodsburg and Mason-Headley Roads. On July 30, 1950, construction was started on the 130-room Campbell House. Pictures of the Campbell House are in Chapter 4.

A current photo of the building at 124 East Main Street.

A current photograph of the northwest building at Martin Luther King Boulevard and East Main Street.

The Post Office and U.S. Custom House were located at Walnut and East Main Streets. This building was replaced by the Federal Building at Barr and Limestone Streets, that is seen in Chapter 2.

The Post Office stood at Walnut Street, now Martin Luther King Blvd., and East Main Street. Lawyers' and architects' offices now occupy this location.

The Post Office building and U.S. Custom House at Walnut Street and East Main Street are shown on a postcard that was sent in July, 1907. $2-8

The current location where the Post Office formerly stood, on East Main Street and near Martin Luther King Blvd.

Another view of the Post Office building, showing the buildings on Walnut Street, on a postcard that was sent in August, 1909. $3-8

A photograph of the northeast corner of East Main Street and Martin Luther King Blvd.

Johns Drug Store was located at Main and Walnut Streets where C.A. Johns constructed his store in 1888. He continued in that location until the 1930s.

A postcard view of John's Drug Store at Main and Walnut Streets. *On loan*.

East Main Street, as seen from Martin Luther King Blvd.

An East Main Street postcard view, looking towards the Fayette Bank building, was sent in January, 1924. $4-8

A current photograph of East Main Street from Martin Luther King Boulevard.

The Kentucky Theatre and Hotel Lafayette were on the left of East Main Street, while the Post Office and Johns Drug Store were on the right side.

A postcard view looking from East Main Street towards the Fayette Bank Building was mailed in September, 1928. The message from Lexington stated, "I was told to write you. So now it is your turn to write me."

A photo of East Main Street as seen from Martin Luther King Blvd.

A 1970s postcard shows East Main Street looking towards the former Fayette Bank Building.

A postcard view on East Main Street looking towards the former Fayette Bank building. This newer postcard was not sent, but was inscribed, "Main Street Lexington, Ky, the heart of the Bluegrass country. The main business section of the modern city, is the trading center for 500,000 people. Founded in 1774, Lexington is home to University of KY." $1-3

The former location of the Phoenix Hotel is where the Lexington Public Library, Park Plaza Apartment Building, and Phoenix Park now are.

A current view of the location of the former Phoenix Hotel, now the Lexington Public Library.

Judge J. H. Mulligan first read his poem "In Kentucky," at the Phoenix Hotel, on February 11, 1902, for a banquet for members of the Kentucky legislature. *The Lexington Leader* ran the poem on its front page the next day, and described the Judge's reading of his poem in this way: "As if drawing a deadly weapon, and peering over his glasses with a smile of satisfaction that amounted to almost a leer, ...he read the poem, which was constantly interrupted by applause that burst into a grand napkin salute at its close."

The Morning Herald reported that "the service was so bad that much of the pleasure of the evening was spoiled and it would have been a failure had it not been for the speeches and that Judge Mulligan for a quarter of hour kept the house in a continual uproar" with his poem.

The current Lexington Public Library.

A postcard view of the Phoenix Hotel that was mailed on April, 1910. $3-8

A view inside the Phoenix Hotel. $1-3

A postcard view of the Phoenix Hotel that was mailed in June, 1934. $2-3

This postcard view of a new coffee shop in the Phoenix Hotel was mailed in August, 1939. The back of the card is inscribed, "1797-Postlewarth Inn-1920, The Phoenix Hotel successor, a hostelry continuously on the same site since 1797. $1-3

Current picture of where the Union Railroad Station existed. This is the location of Fayette County Clerk and Drivers License Offices.

A current view of the Union Railroad Station location.

The Union Depot as shown on a postcard that was mailed August 10, 1914, and was published by Wrenn & King. It is inscribed, "Hello, Mr. Karl, hon about you, Gee but the beer is good In Lexington, Will take a glass for you, Wonder if you all miss me, don't work Hard, as ever, Margaret. $4-6

The Union Railroad Station shown on a 1930s postcard. $2-3

A more recent view of the Union Railroad Station appears on a 1930 to 1945 postcard.

A current picture of where the Union Railroad Station existed.

The former location of the Union Railroad Station is now the Fayette County Clerk and Drivers License offices.

A more recent view of the Union Railroad Station on another postcard. While it was not sent, it did have advertising, "The Blue Grass region is full of scenic beauty and ....traditional lore." $1-3

East Main across from Union Railroad Station had the Post Office Building, the Drug Store on East Main, Morton School and Central Christian Church on Walnut Street. The Drug Store was constructed in 1888-1889 by C.A. Johns and emained the same until the 1930s when it became Bradley's Drugstore until the 1960s.

The place across from where Union Railroad Station was located now is a bank plaza.

A postcard view of East Main Street, across from the Union Railroad Station. $3-6

On East Main Street past Walnut Street, the Morton School and Ben Snyder's are on the left side, while the Phoenix and Lafayette Hotels are on the right.

A current eastern view on East Main Street looking towards Martin Luther King Blvd.

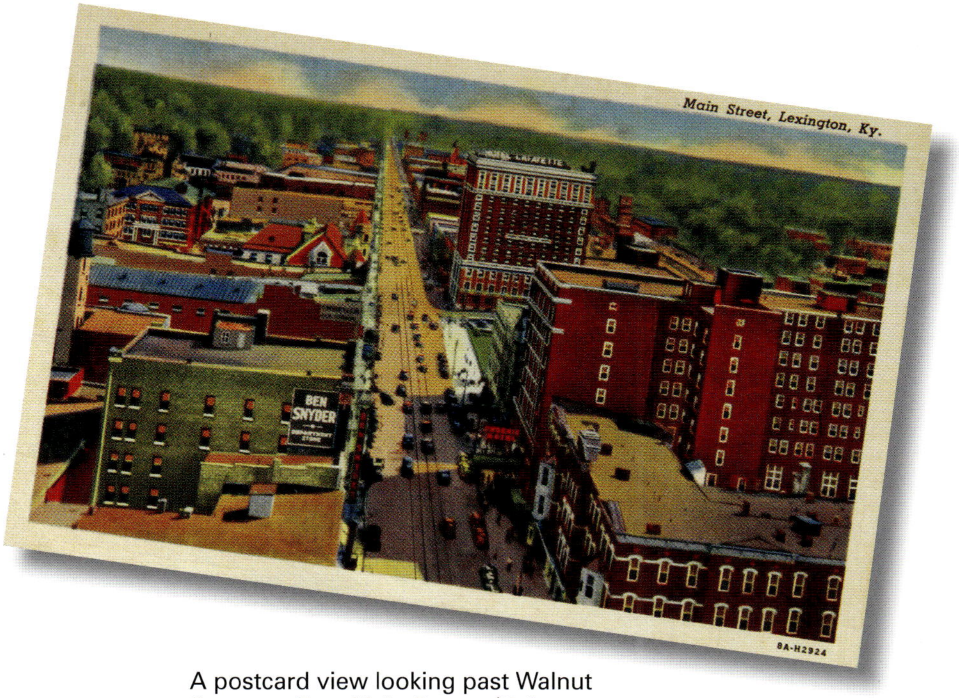

A postcard view looking past Walnut Street on East Main Street. $3-6

The Lexington-Fayette County Government Building was purchased in 1982 from Ashland Oil Company. It was the former location of the Lafayette Hotel from 1920 to 1960.

The Hotel Lafayette was constructed in 1920, and for 40 years was synonymous with warm hospitality in the Bluegrass. It became the headquarters for the Kentucky Central Life Insurance Companies and later became offices for Ashland Oil Company.

The view is of the Lexington Fayette County Government Building.

A postcard shows the Hotel Lafayette. $1-3

Into the Lexington-Fayette County Government Building, Harold Barker, consultant to this book, moved the Lexington City Records and Archives in 1982. The collection had grown so much by 1988 that a larger facility for the Lexington City Records and Archives was needed. Harold continued to maintain those records at the Clark Street Government Building.

A view of the Lexington Fayette County Government Building.

A postcard of the Lafayette Hotel sent in 1923, $1-3.

Inside the Lafayette Hotel around 1930s is shown on a postcard.

A postcard inside view of the Lafayette Hotel $1-2

A view of the Lexington Fayette County Government Building on the left, looking west down Main Street.

The Lexington Fayette County Government Building occupied the former location of The Lafayette Hotel.

A current view of the Lexington Fayette County Government Building.

The Lafayette Hotel, with 300 air-conditioned rooms, included the lobby, Georgian Dining Room, Hunt Room Grill, Cocktail Lounge, and Piano Bar.

A postcard view of the Georgian Dining Room in the Lafayette Hotel. It advertised 300 air conditioned rooms with baths and TV. $2-3

244 East Main Street was formerly the Wolf Wiles Building, now the location of an office.

221-223 East Main Street is the location of Chase Bank Plaza area.

A view of the current building at 244 East Main Street.

The current building at 221-223 East Main Street.

A postcard showing the Greyhound Bus Terminal at 244 East Main Street. *On loan*.

A postcard view of 221-223 East Main Street, Wheeler's, Kentucky's finest furniture store. $3-5

The current apartment building at 347 East Main Street.

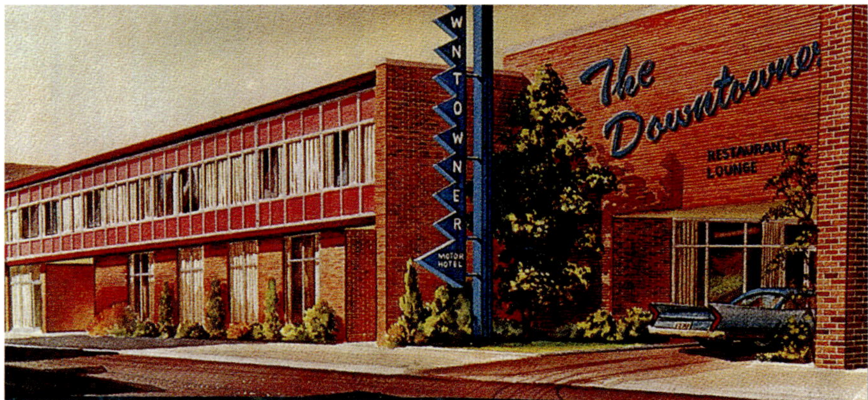

A postcard view showing the Downtowner Motor Hotel on 347 E. Main Street. $2-3

The Downtowner Motor Hotel, at 347 E. Main Street, had 76 air-conditioned units and a swimming pool. A newspaper article related on July 6, 1987, that the Downtowner Motor Inn shut down after 27 years, citing changes in the times and less traffic.

A view of 347 East Main Street.

Downtowner Motor Hotel had 100 air-conditioned rooms, facilities for meetings, private parties, and a convention hall.

The Downtowner Motor Hotel at 347 East Main Street, as seen on a postcard. $1-2

800 East Main Street now is a pizza restaurant.

The current building at 800 East Main Street.

Gen. Roger Williams, of 800 East Main Street, married a daughter of E.D. Sayre, became Brigadier General of the Kentucky State Guard, and was appointed as Adjutant General by the Governor in 1907. He was a well-known soldier, sportsman, and businessman who died on December 15, 1925. He was buried in the Lexington Cemetery.

The home of Gen. Roger Williams, at 800 East Main Street. *On loan*.

Henry Clay's home from 1806-1852, Ashland, was located on the corner at Richmond and Sycamore Roads.

A current picture of Henry Clay's Home located on the corner of East Main Street and Sycamore Road.

A postcard view of Ashland, Henry Clay's home. *On loan*.

The old Henry Clay High School was located at 701 East Main Street. Its buildings are now used for school administration offices. A new Henry Clay High School was built in 1970 on Fontaine Road.

The current view of Henry Clay High School, located at 701 E. Main Street.

Postcard of Henry Clay High School. It was built in 1928 and located at 701 East Main Street.

A postcard view of Henry Clay High School. $4-6

The Idle Hour Country Club is on Richmond Road, an extension of East Main Street.

Idle Hour Country Club

The previous Ashland Golf Club was on Richmond Road.

The Ashland Golf Club. *On loan*.

The current view of Lexington Reservoir, located on Richmond Road.

The Lexington Reservoir and Pumping Station was located just off Richmond Road.

A postcard view of the Reservoir and Pumping Station, sent on Dec. 1910. $2-4

A current picture of the Reservoir on Richmond Road.

A postcard showing the reservoir was mailed in 1910. $1-3

Postcard of Maple Rest Motel Cottages located two miles south of Lexington on U.S. 25.

Two miles south of Lexington, on U.S .Highway 25 at the intersection of routes 60, 27 and 68, is the current location of the Burke Furniture Co. since the 1960s.

A postcard view of the Maple Rest Cottages, advertising "Sleeping in safety and comfort without extravagance," and owned and managed by Mrs. Ella Clark Smith. $1-3

At the Burke Furniture Company, the author and her husband purchased two rooms of office furniture around the 1970s. At that time, the furniture company was using old cottages for storage and she found the Maple Rest Motel postcards and shared them with the owners. This is a typical occurance and the fun of postcard collecting. The furniture is still in use in Florida.

The current location of the Burke Furniture Store, two miles south on U.S. Highway 25, RFD 5.

A postcard view of the Maple Rest Tourist Court, advertising "Rest tourist Homes and cottages by Mrs. George R. Smith." $1-3

US 25 at the intersection of US Highways 60, 27 and 68, the location of Burke Furniture Company. Other businesses have operated on each side of Burke Furniture Co. as the area has continued to grow.

A view of current buildings that appear at the intersection of U.S. Highways 60, 27 and 68.

A recent postcard showing the Maple Rest Cottages, two miles south on U.S. Highway 25, advertising "Maple Rest Tourist Court, Mrs. George R. Smith owner-manager. $1-2

BIBLIOGRAPHY

Allmen, Diane. *Official Price Guide of Postcards*. New York, New York: House of Collectables, 1990.

Bolin, James Duane. *Bossism and Reform in a Southern City: Lexington, Kentucky 1880-1940.* Lexington, Kentucky: University Press of Kentucky, 2000.

Coleman, J. Winston Jr. *The Squire's Sketches of Lexington.* Lexington, Kentucky: Clay Press, 1972.

Deese, Wynelle. *Lexington Kentucky: Changes in the Early Twentieth Century*. Charleston, S.C.: Arcadia Publishing, 1998.

_____. *The Early Gatekeepers: A Saga of Three American Institutions.* Publish America, 2005.

Kerr, Bettie and John Wright. *Lexington: A Century in Photographs.* Lexington, Ky: Lexington-Fayette County Historic Commission, 1984.

Lancaster, Clay. *Vestiges of the Venerable City*. Cincinnati: C.J. Krehbile Co., 1978.

Lexington City Directories, 1900-1960. Lexington-Fayette Urban County Government Archives and Lexington Public Library.

Lexington Local History Index. Lexington Public Library.

Mashburn, J.L. *The Artist Signed Postcard Price Guide*. Alexander, North Carolina: Colonial House Production, 1993.

Miller, George. *The Backbone of the Hobby: Postcard Collector.* 2nd edition. Iola, Wisconsin: Jones Publishing, 1992.

INDEX